Written by
Sylva Nnaekpe

Copyright © 2020 Sylva Nnaekpe.

All rights reserved. No part of this book may be reproduced by any means, medium, graphic, electronic or mechanical, including photocoping, recording, taping or by any information storage retrival system without the written permission of the author except in the case of brief quotations embodied in critical articles and reviews.

Books may be ordered through bookstores or by contacting Silsnorra llc at:
silsnorra@gmail.com

Due to the dynamic nature of the internet, any web address or links contained in this book may have changed since publication and may no longer be valid. The views expressed in this work are solely those of the author and do not necessarily reflect the views of the publisher, and the publisher hereby disclaims any responsibility for them.

ISBN: 978-1-951792-92-3 (Soft Cover)
ISBN: 978-1-951792-93-0 (Hard Cover)
ISBN 978-1-951792-94-7 (Electronic book)
ISBN: 978-1-951792-95-4 (Notebook)

Printing information available on the last page.

Silsnorra llc Review Date: 01/19/2020

"There are times when I have a bad day all day," said Ivry to her friends. "There are times when my day does not go as planned, but I like to have a good day as often as I can. I want to stay fresh, positive, and embrace a life of gratitude. I want to appreciate the things and the people around me.

"What do you mean by a life of gratitude?" asked Jose and Tini, Ivry's friends.

Ivry replied, "A life of gratitude means being thankful for my family, friends, my teachers, my good health, the food I eat, the water I drink, and those who help me succeed. My mum calls them The Great Things of Life, which are so easily ignored."

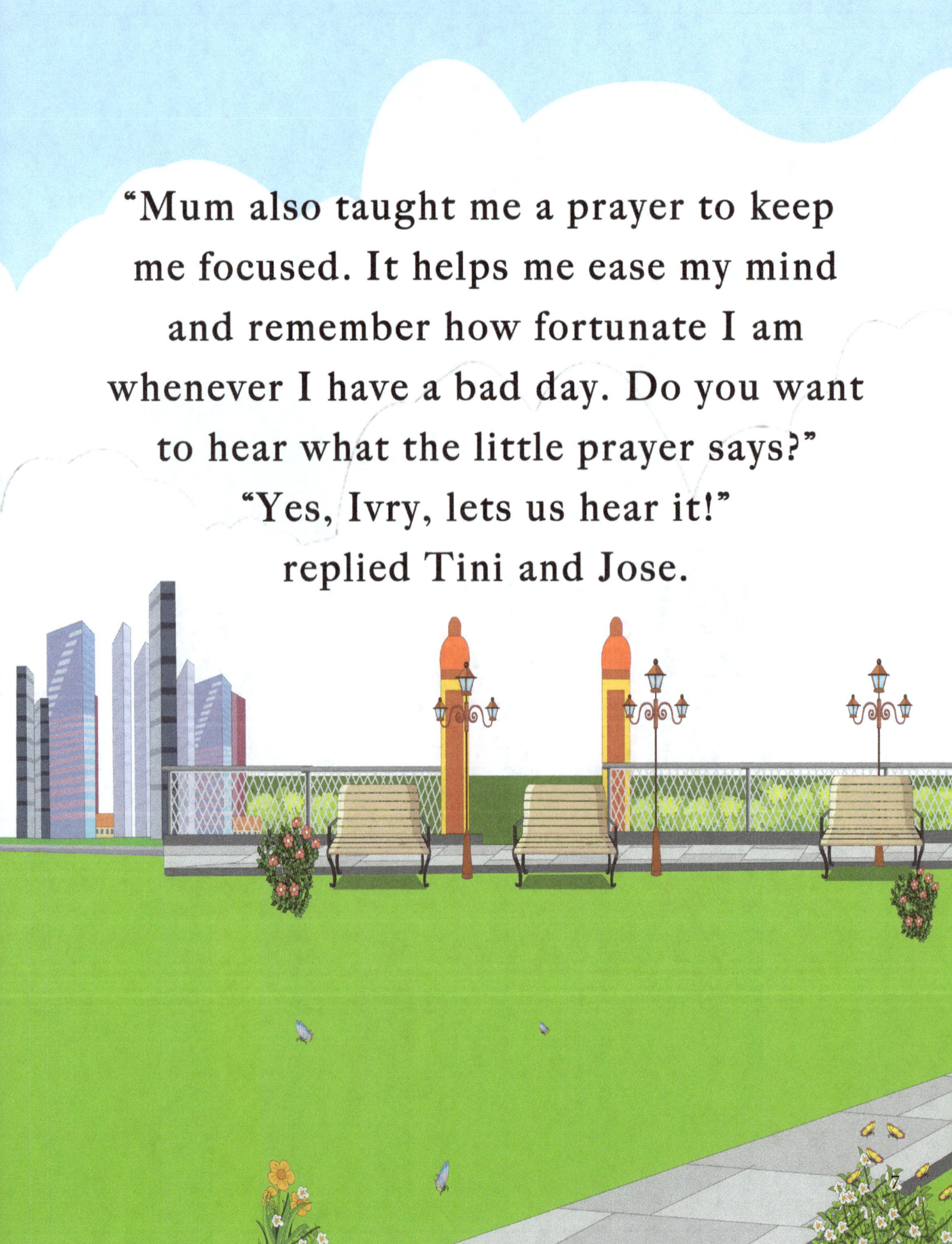

"Mum also taught me a prayer to keep me focused. It helps me ease my mind and remember how fortunate I am whenever I have a bad day. Do you want to hear what the little prayer says?"
"Yes, Ivry, lets us hear it!" replied Tini and Jose.

"Whenever I feel grumpy and begin to act out, I try to focus on happy things, and silently I say, 'God, please refresh my thoughts and fill them with yours.'

"Whenever I am hungry and become irritable, I try to focus on happy things, and silently I say,
'God, please refresh my thoughts and fill them with yours.'

"Whenever I am exhausted but can't take a nap, I try to focus on happy things, and silently I say, 'God, please refresh my thoughts and fill them with yours.'

"Whenever I am worried about something,
do not know how to express myself, or
if I feel sad because no one understands
me, I try to focus on happy things,
and silently I say,
'God, please refresh my thoughts and
fill them with yours.'

"When my friends are mean to me
or don't want to play with me at
school, I try to focus on happy things,
and silently I say,
'God, please refresh my thoughts and
fill them with yours.'

"When I want something but I can't get it because it's not the right time, or because my parents have a lot going on, I try to focus on happy things, and silently I say, 'God, please refresh my thoughts and fill them with yours.'

"When I am afraid and feel uncertain about things, I try to focus on happy things, and silently I say, 'God, please refresh my thoughts and fill them with yours.'

"When I am sad, angry, or have been pushed to my limit, I try to focus on happy things, and silently I say, 'God, please refresh my thoughts and fill them with yours.'

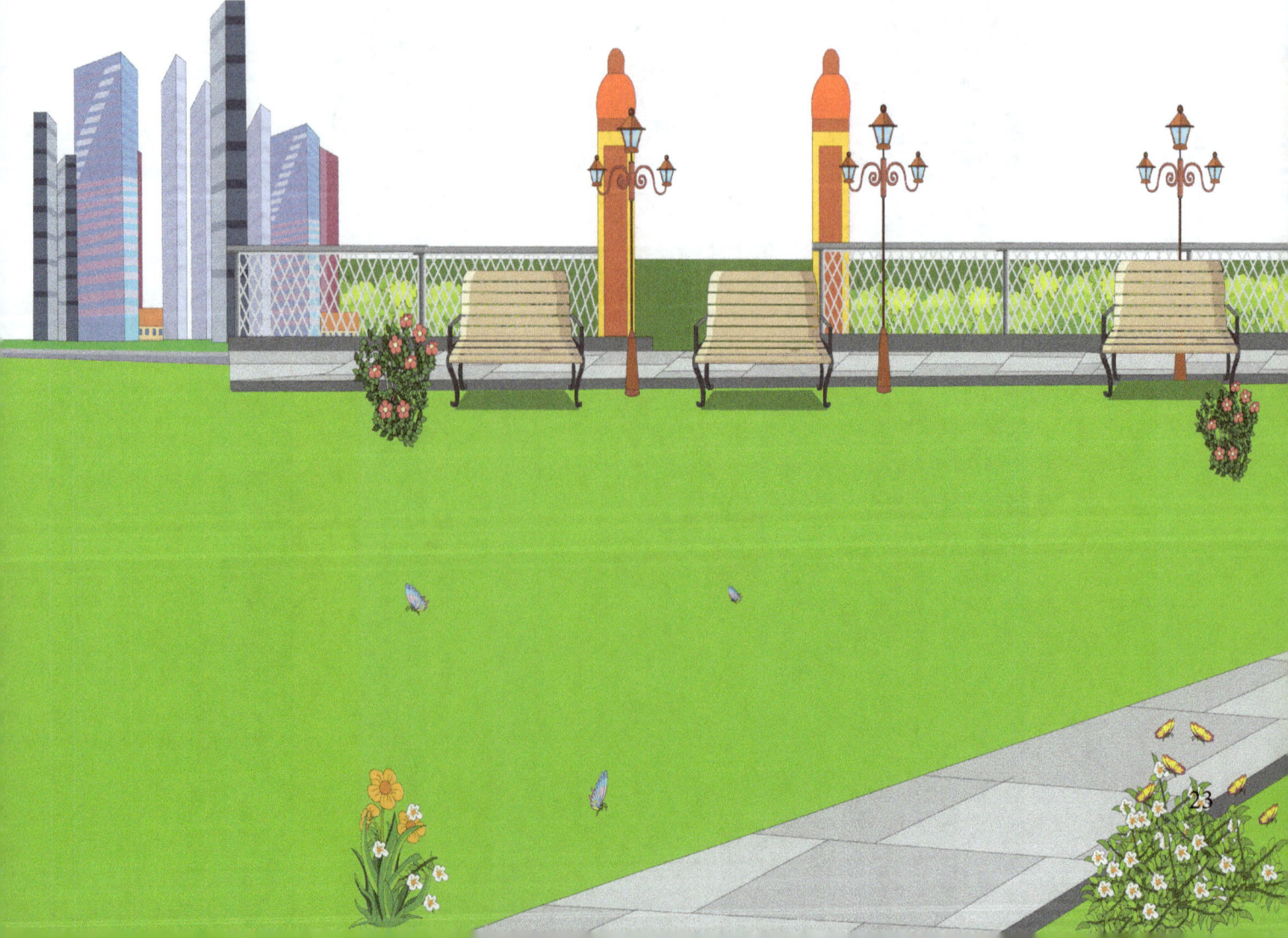

"In the end, it gives me a refreshing feeling of clarity, love, and safety. And guess what? As I focus on this little prayer, those irritable feelings gradually begin to fade away!

Jose, Tini, just remember to focus on happy things whenever you are having a bad day. It will help you get back on track and be happy again.

Remember,
whenever you have a bad day,
say this little prayer:
God, please refresh my thoughts
and fill them with yours."

THE END

Follow @ ivrydbook

to see more.